Fresh Foundations
For
Fresh Living

"Beginning a journey always starts with a recognition for a need to go somewhere."

Ethan Ray

Copyright © 2025 by Ethan Ray

Light Publications

All rights reserved.

This book or parts thereof may not be reproduced in any form, stored in any retrieval system, or transmitted in any form by any means—electronic, mechanical, photocopy, recording, or otherwise—without prior written permission of the publisher, except as provided by United States of America copyright law.

"Scripture quotations taken from the NASB® 1995 - New American Standard Bible®, Copyright © 1960, 1971, 1977,1995 by The Lockman Foundation. Used by permission. All rights reserved. www.Lockman.org"

Acknowledgments

I wish to begin by saying I thank my God for giving me the desire to see growth and discipleship for those new in the faith seeking answers. I thank God for giving me direction in preparing and writing this devotional.

To my sweet wife, **Shelby Ray**. Thank you for all you are to me and all that you do for me. You inspire me each and everyday to be a better Christian, and to be a better man. You mean so much to me, and to have you by my side in ministry, means more than you'll ever know. I love you, Shelby Ray. Thank you for supporting me each day, and for praying for me all the same!

To my supportive **Church family at the Michie Church**. Thank you for your prayers and constant words of encouragement to both me and my family. Thank you for coming alongside us and running this race with us. We are each running in the Steps of Jesus Christ, and I rejoice that I get to do it with each of you.

To my dear friends, **Ryan Napalo, and John Spears**. Thank you both for being such great friends. Friends that always push me to go the extra mile. I believe that everyone needs friends like these in their life, people that are always willing to keep you on your toes, pushing you to do more.

To the **readers and partakers of this devotional**. Thank you for choosing to take the time to step foot into a new life. I shared with my Church at the start of the new year that each of us needed to start our year with a fresh foundation, and to build our faith. That meant that we each needed to build our understanding of Spiritual matters with a strong Biblical basis. I hope that through working these Pillars you will do the same and will be prepared to be a lifelong learner!

I would like to express much gratitude as well to **Bishop Brian Sutton**. Bishop Sutton serves presently as the North American General Presbyter for the Church of God of Prophecy. It was his desire for growth and excellence in the Church that inspired me to write this book. Also, with his assistance and his own book *Join the Journey* I was able to complete *Fresh Foundations for Fresh Living*. Thank you, Bishop Sutton for your continued support and guidance.

Finally, I wish to thank my own State Bishop, **Bishop Paul Holt**, and his wife **Barbara** for their kind words, encouragement, and direction within this book. Their own book, *The Goldfish Principal* inspired what is shared in Chapter 8, and their wisdom helped push me to write this discipleship journey. Thank you both for all you do for me!

- Ethan Ray

Table of Contents

Introduction	7
Pillar 1: A Place to Begin	8
Pillar 2: Fresh Look at the Map	14
Pillar 3: Who is God? Understanding the Trinity	16
Pillar 4: Relationship - Love God and Love People	18
Pillar 5: What Do You See?	20
Pillar 6: It Is More Than Just Emotion	22
Pillar 7: Committed to the Cause	28
Pillar 8: You are the Goldfish	31
Pillar 9: From Milk to Meat	34
Pillar 10: From Journey's Start to Life's Commitment	36
Spiritual Gifts Inventory Tool	40
Additional Resources	46
Statement of Faith	47
Core Values	49
References	50

Introduction - Fresh Foundations for Fresh Living

Beginning a journey always starts with a recognition for a need to go somewhere.
So, Let's Go Somewhere

Objective:

This study is to equip new believers/readers with a solid biblical foundation, an understanding of The Church of God of Prophecy (COGOP) doctrine, and practical pillars for spiritual growth and Church engagement.

Format: Weekly or Monthly sessions (60–90 minutes each), including teaching, discussion, and application.

1 evening a week or month to discuss topics

8-10 Weeks/Months worth of study

Each week/month you will take time with your mentor/teacher to talk through the new pillar placed before you. Why have I used the word pillar for each chapter heading? A pillar is a strong vertical structure that supports a building or holds something up. It can be made of stone, wood, or metal and is often used to bear weight or provide stability from the foundation.

Beyond its physical meaning, pillar is also used symbolically to represent something strong, foundational, and essential. For example:

- In faith, pillars represent core beliefs or principles.
- In communities, a pillar is a respected and influential person.
- In personal growth, pillars can symbolize key values or habits that uphold a strong life.

For you, each week/month your pillar symbolizes a new strong support in your new found faith in Jesus Christ.

I pray that you will handle each pillar with patience and sincerity as you allow the Holy Spirit to lead you into a deeper relationship with God.

- Ethan Ray

Pillar 1: A Place to Begin

From a game of monopoly with the family, to a race in the World Olympics, or the first step in a recipe, there is always a place to begin. The same can be said about our relationship with Christ. We each try so hard to be the next Billy Graham, and then when we fall short we call it quits because we think we have failed. God did not call us all to be Billy Graham. He called you to be you. So, how do I know who I am? I must start from the place that He is, the altar of prayer where I met Him for the first time.

- Ethan Ray

Key Scripture:

Romans 8:1-2

"Therefore there is now no condemnation for those who are in Christ Jesus. For the law of the Spirit of life in Christ Jesus has set you free from the law of sin and of death."

2 Corinthians 5:17

"Therefore if anyone is in Christ, *he is* a new creature; the old things passed away; behold, new things have come."

John 3:16-17

"For God so loved the world, that He gave His only begotten Son, that whoever believes in Him shall not perish, but have eternal life. For God did not send the Son into the world to judge the world, but that the world might be saved through Him."

Topics:

What is the purpose of Salvation?

Where does your understanding of Salvation take you next, how does it become more than just an experience in the altar?

How would you describe a relationship with Christ?

"**Repentance** is the presence and work of the Holy Spirit in the world and upon the human heart through the gospel of Jesus Christ (John 16:8–11) brings CONVICTION, an awareness and acknowledgment of sin against God and the need to confess that guilt with Godly sorrow (2 Corinthians 7:10). In short, repentance means not only being sorry for sin, but a turning from and forsaking the old life (sin habits) for a new walk by faith in God through the Holy Spirit and in company with the people of God (Acts 2:42). The result of repentance is salvation, a work that is both instantaneous (new birth—John 3:3–8) and life-inclusive, beginning with the giving of new life by the Holy Spirit to the believer and climaxing with a glorified body (Hebrews 9:28; Mark 1:15; Luke 13:3; Acts 3:19)" (Biblical 2014).

"**Faith** is confidence in what we hope for and assurance about what we do not see" (Hebrews 11:2).

Grace "or merciful behavior of a more powerful person toward another. Displayed by the Lord toward humankind and by people towards each other in the Old Testament. Used to describe God or Christ in their merciful character or actions toward humankind in the New Testament" (Barry 2016).

Questions for Discussion

- Who is the Church of God of Prophecy (*Resource #1, Pg. 44*)
- What is understood in The Holy Spirit's work in the believer's life? (Romans 8:26)
- Upon conversion, what is the believer's commitment to the body of Christ? (Romans 12:1-5, 1 Corinthians 12:12-27)

Take time as a class to review the Membership Matters Course
In this order

- Lesson 4 - *It's Bigger Than We Are*
- Lesson 3 - *Our Local Church*
- Lesson 2 - *Why Membership?*
- Lesson 5 - What Now?

Use Chapter 1 for reference and greater study material

Take time on your own after the class to review the MM material

"John wrote his first epistle to enable believers in Christ to have assurance of their salvation. "These things I have written to you who believe in the name of the Son of God, so that you may know that you have eternal life." (I John 5:13).

This letter gives us at least six criteria by which we can be certain that we are Christians. Please read the following verses and complete the sentence for each:

I John 1:7. I know that I am a Christian if _____

_____

I John 1:9. I know that I am a Christian if _____

_____

I John 2:3. I know I am a Christian if _____

_____

I John 3:9. I know I am a Christian if _____

_____

I John 3:14. I know I am a Christian if _____

_____

I John 5:10. I know I am a Christian if _____

_____

When you become a new creature in Christ, your life changes in significant ways. The following Scriptures describe different kinds of "fruit" resulting from salvation—what Christ produces in you that is observable to others. Please read these verses and answer the questions that follow:

- Matthew 28:19; I Peter 3:21

What action can believers take that provides external evidence of salvation?

_____

Why is this action important?

_____

Galatians 5:22-23

List the nine characteristics of Christ which the Holy Spirit produces in believers.

(1)_____

(2)_____

(3)_____

(4)_____

(5)_____

(6)_____

(7)_____

(8)_____

(9)_____

Which of those characteristics do you feel is most evident in your life?
_____

In which do you have the most room to grow?
_____

Application:

To attract consumers to a product, advertisements often show living proof that it works. Since you belong to Jesus, YOU are the LIVING PROOF of His power to change lives. You have a unique testimony—it's your Jesus Story. It's a story that only you can tell.

"...Always be prepared to give an answer to everyone who asks you to give the reason for the hope that you have" (I Peter 3:15, NIV). The following exercise will help you get prepared to share your story.

WHO YOU ARE—B.C. AND A.D.:

The cross of Jesus is the dividing line in human history. Events are dated either B.C. (before Christ) or A.D. (after Christ). The personal history of His followers can also be divided into two chapters—B.C.—Their life before they began a relationship with Jesus. A.D.—Their life after Christ came in.

Please complete the following sheet labeled "My Story" using the following three steps:

Step 1: WHO I WAS B.C. (THE OLD ME)

Write one or two paragraphs to describe yourself before you were saved.

Step 2: THE TURNING POINT

Describe what happened when you began your relationship with Jesus. What made you realize that he was the answer? What exactly did you do?

Step 3: WHO I AM A.D. (THE NEW ME)

Describe how you are different since Jesus is living in you. How are your attitudes, your behaviors, and your relationships impacted? Explain how you are growing and changing because Christ is in your life?" (Sutton, 2016).

Who I was B.C. (Before Christ)

The Turning Point (When I met Christ)

Who I was A.D. (After Christ)

Pillar 2: Fresh Look at The Map

The Church of God of Prophecy begins its Biblical Principles, Beliefs, and Practices book this way, "From its beginnings, the Church of God of Prophecy has based its beliefs on "the whole Bible rightly divided." We accept the Bible as God's Holy Word, inspired, inerrant, and infallible. We believe the Bible to be God's written revelation of Himself to mankind and our guide in all matters of faith; therefore, we look to the Bible as our highest authority for doctrine, practice, organization, and discipline." We understand and believe that God's Word from the very start points to Jesus. So, where is our map pointing us through every scripture? The place we should always start - Jesus.

- Ethan Ray

Key Scripture:

2 Timothy 3:16-17

"All Scripture is inspired by God and profitable for teaching, for reproof, for correction, for training in righteousness; so that the man of God may be adequate, equipped for every good work."

Psalm 119:105

"Your word is a lamp to my feet, And a light to my path."

Questions for Discussion:

- What is your earliest recollection of the Bible?
- Is scripture reliable? *I challenge you to go beyond what you have been taught, how do you know?*

(For more in depth study, take time to read and apply information from Lee Strobel's *The Case for Christ.)*

- Going back to our key scriptures, what does 2 Timothy 3:16-17 say the purpose of Scripture is, in your life?

How do you currently read, study, and apply the Bible?

- Take time with your teacher/mentor to prepare a Bible Study plan using the SOAP Method. *Scripture, Observations (Key Details), Application, Prayer*

S_____

O_____

A_____

P_____

In order to understand Scripture better, and to dig deeper, we must go beyond just reading it because we "have to," and we must apply it to our own personal lives. Scripture is broken down into many different important details such as themes or thematic topics (e.g., grace, prayer, suffering.) By doing this, we can research important topics; however, this is not the only means of study.

As shared earlier, "we accept the Bible as God's Holy Word, inspired, inerrant (incapable of being wrong), and infallible (without mistake.) We believe the Bible to be God's written revelation of Himself to mankind and our guide in all matters of faith; therefore, we look to the Bible as our highest authority for doctrine, practice, organization, and discipline."

John 1:1-5 shares this,
"In the beginning was the Word, and the Word was with God, and the Word was God. He was in the beginning with God. All things came into being through Him, and apart from Him nothing came into being that has come into being. In Him was life, and the life was the Light of men. The Light shines in the darkness, and the darkness did not comprehend it."

Application:

Your application for this pillar is to find a daily Bible reading plan, and commit to it. Use the SOAP method while you study the particular scripture provided.

I Challenge you to learn and memorize Psalm 119:33-34 as a daily prayer

Pillar 3: Who is God? Understanding the Trinity

Like most Christian Churches, the Church of God of Prophecy holds a firm Trinitarian belief, affirming that God is one yet exists eternally in three Persons: Father, Son, and Holy Spirit. This doctrine is a foundational aspect of the Church's Statement of Faith and aligns deeply with orthodox Christian teachings. These teachings are affirmed within the historic Christian understanding of the Trinity found in the Nicene Creed:

"We believe in one God, the Father, the Almighty... We believe in one Lord, Jesus Christ, the only Son of God... We believe in the Holy Spirit, the Lord, the giver of life, who proceeds from the Father."

- Ethan Ray

Key Scripture:

Luke 2:21-22

"Now when all the people were baptized, Jesus was also baptized, and while He was praying, heaven was opened, and the Holy Spirit descended upon Him in bodily form like a dove, and a voice came out of heaven, "You are My beloved Son, in You I am well-pleased."

One God, Three Persons

The Church of God of Prophecy believes in one God, who eternally exists in three distinct Persons: Father, Son, and Holy Spirit.

God the Father

- The Father is the Creator of all things, seen and unseen. (Col. 1:16)
- He is the source of divine authority and is worshipped as sovereign over all creation.

Jesus Christ, the Son

- Jesus is the eternally begotten Son of God. (John 3:16)
- He is fully divine and fully human, conceived by the Holy Spirit and born of the virgin Mary.
- He suffered, died, was buried, and rose on the third day.
- He ascended to the right hand of the Father and will return to judge the living and the dead.

The Holy Spirit

- The Holy Spirit proceeds eternally from the Father. (John 15:26)
- He is the Teacher, Comforter, and Giver of spiritual gifts. (John 14)
- His presence empowers believers and the church. (Acts 1:8)
- Speaking in tongues and bearing the fruit of the Spirit are recognized as New Testament signs of being filled with the Holy Spirit. (Acts 2:4)

Questions for Discussion:

- What relational qualities exist between Christ and the Father? (John 5:19)
- What relational qualities exist between the Father and Jesus? (John 5:22)
- Define the relationship between the Father and the Son. (John 8:29)
- In your own words, describe the Holy Spirit's role within the Trinity.

Application:

God exists in a perfect, loving Trinity, we are called to reflect that in our relationships.

This month/week how can you intentionally cultivate a deeper community with others, practicing love, humility, and unity that you haven't already?

Pillar 4: Relationship - Love God and Love People

For many Church goers in the world, just attending Church makes them a Christian. However, on the contrary, going to Church makes you a Christian just as much as sitting in a garage makes you a car. Makes no sense, right? We can not assume that we can coast on our parents or grandparents faith and be fine with God. When we begin to step foot into discipleship, we understand that Jesus is chasing after a genuine relationship with us. Relationship comes with a genuine transformation from who we are into who He wants us to be. We must be willing to pursue that relationship in order to be where He wants us to be.

- Ethan Ray

Key Scripture:

Matthew 12:30-31

"And you shall love the Lord your God with all your heart, and with all your soul, and with all your mind, and with all your strength.' The second is this, 'You shall love your neighbor as yourself.' There is no other commandment greater than these."

I want to begin this pillar with a question...

What is Church to you?

From Christian historian Dr. Robert Webber

- *"The Church started as a missionary movement in Jerusalem.*
- *It moved to Rome and became an institution.*
- *It traveled to Europe and became a culture.*
- *It crossed the Atlantic to America and became a big business.*

I didn't even realize how lost I was until I saw what the church was really supposed to look like. At first, I didn't recognize it; then I wanted to rationalize it. I had to go halfway around the world to find it - in the persecuted underground house church in Asia" (Webber, 2007).

When we begin to understand what/who the Church is, we can begin to take a step deeper into what we then do. This Pillar has everything to do with Loving God and Loving People. We love God, so we want to keep His commandments and be in His House. God's people love me, so I can assume they want me to keep God's commandments. That comes from a place of accountability in love.

Questions for Discussion:

- What is the importance of fellowship and accountability?
- What is the purpose of worship, communion, and church gatherings?
- What is the Church's role in society?

The Church is not merely a building or an organization; it is the body of believers who come together in faith, worship, and service to God. In the context of the Church of God of Prophecy, the Church is seen as an essential institution established by God to carry out His mission on earth.

The Church is where:

- **Ministry takes place** – including preaching, teaching, and serving communities.
- **Believers are equipped for leadership** – through structured programs and classes.
- **Doctrine and faith are upheld** – The Church should maintain the structural integrity of Biblical teachings, ensuring that members and attendees are grounded in sound doctrine.
  - **Evangelism** - The Church spreads the gospel globally.
  - **Social Impact** – Through outreach, and community service
  - **Moral Guidance** – The Church provides ethical and moral teachings based on Scripture.

Application:

This month/week apply this pillar to your own life, and be the living and breathing Church.

- In some way 'Love People' the way Christ would and serve them.

Be Ready to Share next meeting

Pillar 5: What Do You See?

For me, growing up in the Church of God of Prophecy meant growing up in what today is called 'Children's Ministries,' but then was called, 'Gleaners.' During my time as a gleaner, we learned the old song, "Be Careful Little Eyes What You See," and the song continued with, "There's a Father up above looking down in tender love, oh be careful little eyes what you see." This song has deep meanings today in our Church culture. (*Note for the Leader* - this particular session can be taken in many different directions. Follow the Spirit for your class.) For many of us, what we have seen, listened to, and grown up around has affected our 'worldview,' and it has formed who we are today. This Pillar takes a look at who you are and what you see.

- Ethan Ray

Key Scripture:

1 Corinthians 2:12-14

"Now we have received, not the spirit of the world, but the Spirit who is from God, so that we may know the things freely given to us by God, which things we also speak, not in words taught by human wisdom, but in those taught by the Spirit, combining spiritual *thoughts* with spiritual *words*. But a natural man does not accept the things of the Spirit of God, for they are foolishness to him; and he cannot understand them, because they are spiritually appraised."

Questions for Discussion:

- What is your worldview?
    - Explain it and how you formed it.
- How do you know right from wrong?

Each of the questions above are different and they provide a place of deep introspection; however, each answer affects our worldview, or in a deeper sense, our Spiritual view. The very first question, "What is your worldview?" is a very difficult question to answer, and many of us do not have an answer. However, within this Pillar, I hope you will gain a new found knowledge of your Spiritual Worldview in your Church.

What is a Spiritual Worldview?

- Seeing the world through the lens of faith and choosing to acknowledge God's sovereignty over all aspects of life (Colossians 1:16-17). This is led by the Spirit's guidance under complete personal discernment.
- Having a worldview that is rooted in God's Word as the final authority (2 Timothy 3:16-17). This is seeing through the complete Authority of Scripture.
- Like the first one, The Holy Spirit is the guide for complete truth and all discernment (John 16:13). The Holy Spirit must direct us and show us all things according to Scripture.
- Having a Kingdom View. A Spiritual Worldview acknowledges the advancement of God's Kingdom as the Church's primary mission (Matthew 6:33).
- On Mission, even in the secular world. You must choose to stand firm in your faith each and every day as a person of utmost integrity.

What does a Spiritual Worldview look like? What has happened when you gained a Spiritual View?

What does church look like from a Spiritual View?

What should church look like from a Spiritual View?

Application

Take a moment and ask yourself the question, "Do I make decisions based on faith, God's Word, the Holy Spirit's direction, and with a Kingdom View, or do I rely solely on my own human reasoning?

Take a moment and personally write where you can do better and how

_____

_____

_____

_____

_____

_____

Pillar 6: It is More Than Just Emotion

I can recall the night that I got saved, I was at Kamp Kumbaya in Eupora, Mississippi. This is also where sanctification began, and I received the Baptism of the Holy Spirit. The night I got saved, I remember spending a lot of time in the altar just crying without actually speaking and using words. Don't get me wrong, sometimes it's sweet to just cry in the Presence of God, but was I actually confessing or letting anything go with those tears? No, I was not. God requires some action from us; it can't always just be emotion. To be in a relationship, you have to put in the work.

- Ethan Ray

Key Scripture:

1 Timothy 4:6-8

"In pointing out these things to the brethren, you will be a good servant of Christ Jesus, *constantly* nourished on the words of the faith and of the sound doctrine which you have been following. But have nothing to do with worldly fables fit only for old women. On the other hand, discipline yourself for the purpose of godliness; for bodily discipline is only of little profit, but godliness is profitable for all things, since it holds promise for the present life and *also* for the *life* to come."

Topics:

Understanding holiness and sanctification.

The power of the Holy Spirit in overcoming sin.

Continual Growth as a Christian.

Spiritual disciplines.

Questions for Discussion:

- What is your understanding of holiness and sanctification?
- What are Spiritual Disciplines?

According to the COGOP Doctrine

Holiness is a command of our Lord: "Be ye holy; for I am holy" (1 Peter 1:14–16), the state of being free from sin (sin's dominance) made possible by God's sanctifying and cleansing work (Romans 6:11–14; 1 Corinthians 6:11), and further sustained by active, whole-hearted pursuit of a life of Christ-likeness on the part of the maturing believer... Holiness must also be the Church's collective goal as the body of Christ to demonstrate the praises (virtues) of Him "who hath called [us] out of darkness into his marvellous light" (1 Peter 2:9, 10)" (Biblical 2014).

Sanctification, like salvation, ultimately spans the entire life of the believer. Initially, it is a work of grace subsequent to being justified, regenerated, or born again. It is an instantaneous work, which both sets one apart for God (1 Corinthians 1:2) and crucifies and cleanses the old nature, enabling the believer to be free from the dominant rule of sin: "Knowing this, that our old man is crucified with him, that the body of sin might be destroyed, that henceforth we should not serve sin. For, he that is dead is freed from sin" (Romans 6:6, 7)...There is then in sanctification, a responsibility on the part of the believer to "put off" some habits and practices, and to "put on" others, which means there must be intentionality to holiness (Ephesians 4:22–32). Sanctification empowers us against sin's control; the believer responds with a renewed mind to be transformed into the image of Christ (Romans 12:1, 2) and to be holy in life and conduct (2 Corinthians 7:1)" (Biblical 2014).

So, How do I continue to grow?

"Commit to Growing in Faith

Faith is the foundation of the entire Christian life (Hebrews 11:6).

- What is faith? (Read Hebrews 11:1)

1. Faith (noun)— "faith, belief, firm persuasion, assurance, firm conviction, honesty, integrity, faithfulness, truthfulness."

2. Believe (verb)— "to trust in; put faith in; rely on a person, or thing; have a mental persuasion; to entrust, commit; to change or power of.

- What is the source of true faith?

The only source of true biblical faith is the Word of God. "Faith cometh by hearing...the Word (Rhema) of God" (Romans 10:4, 16, 17).

In relation to faith, how do we appropriate God's Word?

1. Locate the promise in God's Word that fits the need (Philippians 4:19).
2. Fulfill all of the conditions attached to that need (Isaiah 1:19-20).
3. With patience accept the trying of your faith and God's testing of your faith in the Word (Psalms 105:19; Hebrews 6:12-15; James 1:3, 4).
4. We must firmly and positively claim the fulfillment of the promise and our confession should always be in harmony with God's Word (Hebrews 3:1; 2 Peter 1:3, 4; 1 John 5:14).

Actively appropriating faith is one of the keys to a victorious Christian life!

Commit to Growing in Prayer

Prayer is the key to all spiritual victory.

- **Why should believers pray?**
1. Prayer is not an option (Isaiah 56:7).
2. We are to pray without ceasing (Romans 1:9; 1 Thessalonians 5:17).
3. All men everywhere are to pray (1 Timothy 2:8).
- **What is prayer?**
1. Prayer is a discipline. It is bending the will of man before God to admit his need (2 Chronicles 7:14; Matthew 6:9, 10).
2. Prayer is rendering homage to an all-wise and benevolent heavenly Father (Psalms 108:5).
3. Prayer is spending time in conversation with God. Conversation is a two-way communication.

"But you, when you pray, go into your inner room, close your door and pray to your Father who is in secret, and your Father who sees *what is done* in secret will reward you." (Matthew 6:6).

- **What should be our attitude in prayer?**
1. We should pray in faith (Hebrews 11:6).
2. We should pray without wavering (Mark 11:24; James 1:6-8).
3. We should pray according to God's will (1 John 5:14-16).
4. We should come to the Father through Jesus Christ, our intercessor (Hebrews 7:25).
- **What are the various types of prayers?**
1. Persevering prayer (Luke 11:5-13; Philippians 4:6).
2. Intercessory prayer (Romans 8:26, 27).
3. In the Spirit (1 Corinthians 14:14; Ephesians 6:18; Jude 20).
4. Supplication (1 Timothy 2:1, 2).
5. Giving thanks (Philippians 4:6).
- **Who can be involved in prayer?**
1. Individuals (Matthew 6:5-7).
2. Two or three (Matthew 18:19-20).
3. A whole church (Acts 2:42; 4:24). When the church comes together, it is scriptural for all to lift up their voices in one accord in prayer, praise, and thanksgiving (Psalms 18:6; 64:1; 66:19).

Committed to Growing by Transformation (Sanctification)

- **The God who made us in His image is holy, and He commands us to be holy (Leviticus 19:2; 1 Peter 1:16).**

Jesus became like us that we might be like Him (John 17:17, 20).

- **How does God make us holy?**
    - Faith comes by hearing the Word (Romans 10:17).
    - The Blood of Christ preached.
    - We hear in faith.
    - We are regenerated and joined to Christ.
    - Indwelling of the Spirit gives us power to resist sin and walk in the light.
- **As we submit to the searching and leading of the Holy Spirit by the Word . . .**
    - We find holdouts to our old will.
    - Contrary desires.
    - Confess sins
    - Mortify deeds of the flesh (Galatians 5:24).
    - Walk in the light.
    - Grow in grace.

When there are no more holdouts or resistances, no more ungodly desires or inclination of our hearts to rebel, we experience the purity and holiness of heart, which is Christian perfection (Romans 2:29; 1 Thessalonians 5:23; Hebrews 6:1; 1 John 1:5-7).

- **Problems of the Flesh**

Our problem is not the body, but the "flesh" or human nature that is inclined to rebel against God. God will resurrect the body, the question is, "What to do with the flesh?"

- **We are still fallible, temptable in understanding, temperament, and development by the Fall and its effects on the whole creation and us.**
    - But we have cleansed the deeds of the flesh and spirit and now live in the perfecting walls with a pure heart of love to God and others (2 Corinthians 7:1).
    - If we violate this integrity of heart and life, we experience defilement and distance from God.
    - As we walk with this integrity, we experience clearness and closeness.
    - Galatians 5:25.
    - There is now not only an avoidance of evil, but also a positive seeking and delighting in all of the known will of God (Ephesians 3:17-19).
    - Christ came to secure for all those who trust in Him, the experience of power by His blood.

We must seek God in the altar to mortify the deeds of the flesh and put off the "old man" of sin. To experience the freedom from actual and indwelling sin is our goal. Sanctification is subsequent to the "New Birth," and "Spirit baptism" is subsequent to a clean heart. We must crucify the flesh and allow the blood of Christ to cleanse us daily from all unrighteousness (1 John 1:9)" (Sutton, 2016).

We must allow the Holy Spirit to change our lives. There is more to our relationship with Christ than a single experience (not to diminish the Miracle of Salvation) and tears in the altar. We are called to so much more. Through the life-altering process of Sanctification, the Holy Spirit is able to completely change everything about who we are in our Adamic nature.

Spiritual Disciplines

Celebration of Discipline: The Path to Spiritual Growth by Richard J. Foster shares this, "The classical Disciplines of the spiritual life call us to move beyond surface living into the depths... God intends for the Disciplines of the spiritual life to be for ordinary human beings: people who have jobs, who care for children, who wash dishes and mow lawns... The Spiritual Disciplines are God's means of grace by which we are enabled to bring our little, individualized power pack we call the human body and place it before God as a 'living sacrifice'" (Foster 2018).

The Spiritual Disciplines are what allow us to grow in our relationship with Christ. They are what make our faith more than just emotion in the altar.

Application

"...discipline yourself for the purpose of godliness." 1 Timothy 4:7

This week, include each of these into your daily life. Spend time in Prayer, Study the Word of God, Fast, Find someone to Serve in some capacity, and Worship.

Prayer - Perpetual communion with the Father

Study - The act or experience of analytically explicating (breaking) a subject.

Fasting - *According to Scripture* abstaining from food for spiritual purposes

Service - Humbly serving those around you, expecting nothing in return

Worship - Our response to the love of God - Surrender

Remember, Spiritual Growth Takes Time

Progress not perfection - Trust in Christ

Pillar 7: Committed to the Cause

When I began to sit and think of this Pillar, the thought came to me, *Committed to Christ means you are Committed to the Cause.* So what does that even mean? Well, this Pillar I hope you dive deeper into that idea, but to simplify what I am meaning I will say, in order to be a Christian you must be devoted regardless of the outcomes or circumstances. It is like a relationship or marriage. You make a commitment to your spouse to be devoted in sickness and in health, richer or for poorer, and for better or for worse. You are committed through it all! The same should be said about our relationship with Christ, we are committed regardless of what the devil throws our way.

- Ethan Ray

Key Scripture:

Colossians 3:23-24

"Whatever you do, do your work heartily, as for the Lord rather than for men, knowing that from the Lord you will receive the reward of the inheritance. It is the Lord Christ whom you serve."

Questions for Discussion:

- How does your daily life reflect your devotion to Christ? (Romans 12:1-2)
- What exactly is The Great Commission? (Matthew 28:16-20)
- Why is it important for Christians to share the gospel? (Romans 10:14-15)
- How can we share the gospel effectively in our everyday interactions? (1 Peter 3:15)

The Great Commision - Matthew 28:16-20

"But the eleven disciples proceeded to Galilee, to the mountain which Jesus had designated. When they saw Him, they worshiped *Him*; but some were doubtful. And Jesus came up and spoke to them, saying, "All authority has been given to Me in heaven and on earth. Go therefore and make disciples of all the nations, baptizing them in the name of the Father and the Son and the Holy Spirit, teaching them to observe all that I commanded you; and lo, I am with you always, even to the end of the age."

Here in Matthew 28, we see Jesus tell his disciples what to do. He gives them a "job," a "task," or as the Church of God of Prophecy proclaims a " Mission."

During the 102nd International Assembly of the Church in 2024, the mission statement of "On Mission" was presented to the Church as our directive for the next 2 years. This statement comes from the Latin term *Missio Dei*, which means "The Mission of God" or "The Sending of God." This theme or mission statement aligns with the vision given to the Church body, "Reconciling the World to Christ Through the Power of the Holy Spirit," which was developed and presented to the Church in 2020 by Bishop Sam Clements.

You should not just aspire to be a disciple of Christ and a sharer of the Gospel just because our Church Doctrine says to, but because the Word of God, as we discussed in Pillar two, is inspired, inerrant, and infallible, tells you to. The Bible is God's written revelation of Himself to mankind and our guide in all matters of faith.

Membership of the Church of God of Prophecy

Please read the following scriptures and complete the statement for each:

1. Membership identifies a person as a genuine
_____.
(Romans 12:5; Ephesians 2:19).

2. Membership provides spiritual family to _____ and _____ you in your walk with Christ. (Galatians 6:1-2; Hebrews 10:24-25).

3. Membership gives you a place to discover and use your _____ in _____. (1 Corinthians 12:4-27).

4. Membership places you under the spiritual _____ of godly leaders. (Acts 20:28-29; Hebrews 13:17).

5. Membership gives you _____ you need to grow. (Ephesians 4:12, 13).

Application

- Take time with your group to discuss what it means to Commit to Christ and Commit to this Church.

Our creator designed us to live in relationship with others. In His infinite wisdom, Christ left a pattern for His followers to be joined together. "So we, being many, are one body in Christ, and every one members one of another" (Romans 12:5).

Pillar 8: You are the Goldfish

Tennessee State Bishop, Paul Holt, and his wife Barbara wrote a book that was published in 2022 called "The Goldfish Principle." This book is about the topic of Biblical Stewardship. I highly recommend this book for money management from a Biblical viewpoint. They share, "Some people will always be in debt and short of money regardless of the size of their paycheck because with every increase in income, they increase their spending. The bigger the tank (income), the bigger the fish (spending)" (Holt, 2022). So let's explore this in this Pillar, *You are the Goldfish*.

- Ethan Ray

Key Scripture:

1 Peter 4:10

"As each one has received a *special* gift, employ it in serving one another as good stewards of the manifold grace of God."

Topics:

Biblical principles of giving and generosity.

Managing time for spiritual growth.

Questions for Discussion:

- Is Stewardship just about money?
- How would you describe what stewardship is?

From the Church of God of Prophecy Core Values

"The fourth core value of the Church of God of Prophecy is Biblical Stewardship. The Church affirms that everything belongs to God. While He has graciously entrusted individuals with the care, development, and utilization of His resources. Christians are responsible to manage His holdings well and according to His desires and purposes.

The Church acknowledges and encourages its members to recognize they are stewards of the resources, abilities, and opportunities God has entrusted to them, and one day, each one will be called to give an account for how what the Master gave was managed. Therefore, it is with joy that the Church works hand-in-hand with God, utilizing that which God had given, to His glory and honor" (Biblical).

As a group, read and discuss Matthew 25:14-30

- What was the significance of the third servant hiding his talent in the ground rather than using it? *How can we relate this action to our own fears, doubts, or inaction in serving God?*
- What does the master's reaction to the third servant's actions teach us about accountability? *What does the statement "you knew that I reap where I have not sown" mean in the context of the parable?*

Barbara Holt shares these steps in their book within chapter 5 *Creating a Plan,* "**Step One:** Make God First Priority. **Step Two:** Realize that God owns everything. **Step Three:** Accept the responsibility of being a manager. **Step Four:** Take a look at your whole financial picture" (Holt, 2022).

While I do want you to succeed at financial management, stewardship is more than just money. Stewardship is "being responsible to manage God's holdings well and according to His desires and purposes." You need a plan, like the one above, and you need to commit to it as we did in Pillar 7.

Application:

On your own time, on a separate paper, work through each of these

1. Your own Personal Reflection on Resources:

    Assess how you are using your time, talents, and treasures. How can you be more intentional in stewarding these resources in a way that honors God?

2. Serving Others:

    Stewardship isn't just about managing resources for yourself, but also about using those resources to bless others. What are opportunities to serve in the community or church, whether through volunteering, donating, or offering time and skills to help those in need can you see?

3. Financial Stewardship:

    If you do not currently have a budget, create one. Reach out to your pastor or a mentor for help. Find a way to bless God first within your giving.

4. Time Management:

    How do you spend your time? Are you being a good steward of your day? Could you spend more time in prayer, studying Scripture, or serving others? Tell me how.

5. Accountability:

    Find a partner or group to hold each other accountable in being faithful stewards. This is for, finances if need, service, and time with God

Pillar 9: From Milk to Meat

1 Corinthians 3:2 says this, "I gave you milk to drink, not solid food; for you were not yet able *to receive it*. Indeed, even now you are not yet able." This devotional of 10 Pillars is to be used as a stepping stone material. This is an introduction of basic discipleship materials needed to move deeper in the word. What is included within each Pillar is not everything that the Word of God has to offer, but a drop in the bucket around each subject that I felt led to share. Paul is speaking to the Church at Corinth as I am speaking to you, drink the milk but don't live on it. Once you have finished these last two chapters - begin taking new bites of meat. You are ready for fresh living!

- Ethan Ray

Key Scripture:

James 1:2-4

"Consider it all joy, my brethren, when you encounter various trials, knowing that the testing of your faith produces endurance. And let endurance have *its* perfect result, so that you may be perfect and complete, lacking in nothing."

Topics:

There is power in prayer and fasting - you must have faith.

Going deep means understanding that trusting God goes beyond good moments.

Questions for Discussion:

- What do you consider the meat?
- Why do Christians suffer? (Romans 5:3-5)
- What does it mean to be truly devoted to God? (Luke 9:23)

When I sit and think about trials, and suffering as Christians - I think of my late grandmother, Evanell Garrison. My mawmaw was a Pastor's Wife, and she was a great one. Her life, however, was not always great. She grew up in a very poor home and faced many of the same challenges in her adult married life. My grandfather was an alcoholic when they married, and she faced many challenges in their first many years of marriage. She, however, never lost her faith and kept praying and attending Church. She became a member of the Church of God and was filled with the Baptism of the Holy Spirit which only amplified her faith. Fast forward, my grandfather received salvation and the Baptism of the Holy Spirit, and he became an Anointed Preacher and Pastor. Their story of suffering did not stop there, but I will spare the time and share one story.

They were very poor, and in need of money to feed themselves and their 5 children. Without food for breakfast or lunch one Sunday, they went on to Church in faith that God would take care of them. When they returned home from Church that day, their entire table was full of groceries. This was due to a real faith in God, not a comfortable cultural Christianity. Their faith went beyond just milk and into the meat of the Spirit. They knew that God would take care of them, and He did.

Deeper Study

- Why does God sometimes allow us to face difficult circumstances in life, and how can we find the "meat" of His Word in those times?
- How does spiritual maturity change our understanding and application of Scripture? How do we go beyond just skimming the surface?
- What does it look like to grow in spiritual maturity, and how can we help others move toward the "meat" of God's Word in their own lives? How can discipleship help others go deeper into their faith?
- How do we stay rooted in the "meat" of God's Word amidst distractions and challenges in life? What habits or disciplines can we put in place to ensure we're constantly growing in our understanding of God's truth?

Application: *Be real with your group*

In what areas of your own life do you need to submit to God? Where are you drinking milk?

Take time to share a testimony of faith when God showed up in your life.

Pillar 10: From Journey's Start to Life's Commitment

As I shared at the start of Pillar 9, " This devotional of 10 Pillars is to be used as a stepping stone material. This is an introduction of basic discipleship materials needed to move deeper in the Word. What is included within each Pillar is not everything that the Word of God has to offer, but a drop in the bucket around each subject that I felt led to share." From this Pillar, you are ready to begin "Fresh Living" in your relationship with Christ. It can't be a resolution that you decide to quit later when it gets hard, but from today forward you must walk in a new life. You must walk committed to your relationship with Christ.

- Ethan Ray

Key Scripture:

Joshua 1:9

"Have I not commanded you? Be strong and courageous! Do not tremble or be dismayed, for the Lord your God is with you wherever you go."

Topics:

The importance of perseverance in faith.

Staying connected and growing in the church.

Developing a personal discipleship plan.

Spiritual Gifts in the Church.

Questions for Discussion: *Elaborate on more than just the Scripture - provide your own thoughts*

- Why is it important to actively grow your faith and understanding? (Hebrews 11:6)
- Why do we need Church? Why do we go to Church?
- Do you have a personal Discipleship plan for after this meeting? **Create one**

Our Church has a desire to see leaders grow, and develop into what God wants for them. There is a commitment to training and raising up individuals who will lead and serve for the next generation. You may not be called to be a Pastor, or an Evangelist, or a Leader in the Church, but God does call you to be a knowledgeable Christian. 2 Peter 3:18 says this, "But grow in the grace and knowledge of our Lord and Savior Jesus Christ. To Him be the glory, both now and to the day of eternity. Amen." As Christians, we are to gain all that we can from the Word of God and also in our personal studies. I challenge you today, be a committed life long learner of God.

Spiritual Gifts According to:

1 Corinthians 12:4-11

- Wisdom
- Knowledge
- Faith
- Healing
- Miracles
- Prophecy
- Discerning of spirits
- Tongues
- Interpretation of tongues

Romans 12:6-8

- Prophecy
- Service
- Teaching
- Exhortation
- Giving
- Leadership
- Mercy

5 Fold Ministry "for the equipping of the saints for the work of service"(Ephesians 4:11-12)

- Apostles
- Prophets
- Evangelists
- Pastors
- Teachers

Notes

Resources
For
Spiritual Growth

&

Leadership
Development

Spiritual Gifts Inventory Tool

Please complete the Spiritual Gifts Inventory Tool below. Through this tool, I have hope that you will find what God has equipped you to do in service for Him; and I hope that through this you will engage in ministry both in your local church and in building God's kingdom.

Instructions:
There are a total of 110 statements below. Please indicate whether you Strongly Agree, Agree Somewhat, Undecided, Disagree Somewhat, or Completely Disagree with each question.
Transfer your answers to the profile sheet at the end of this document.
Total your scores for each of the gifts. Each gift will have a score between ZERO and TWENTY.
Order the gifts in descending order of score. Higher scores indicate your more dominant gifts.

- 4 – Strongly Agree
- 3 – Agree Somewhat
- 2 – Undecided
- 1 – Disagree Somewhat
- 0 – Completely Disagree

1. People seem to be willing to follow my leadership without much resistance. 1._____
2. I like to proclaim God's Word to fellow Christians. 2._____
3. It is a joy for me to proclaim God's plan of salvation to unchurched people 3._____
4. It is enjoyable to have the responsibility of leading other people in their spiritual life. 4._____
5. I'm excited by helping people to discover important truths in the scriptures. 5._____
6. I have special joy singing praises to God either alone or with other people. 6._____
7. It is enjoyable to motivate people to a higher spiritual commitment. 7._____
8. People with spiritual problems seem to come to me for advice and counsel. 8._____
9. I received excellent grades in school. 9._____
10. There is great joy in doing little jobs around the church. 10._____
11. I look for opportunities to assist people in their work. 11._____
12. There is great joy in leading people to accomplish group goals. 12._____
13. I like to organize people for more effective ministry. 13._____
14. There is great satisfaction in giving large amounts of money for the Lord's work. 14._____
15. I feel great compassion for the problems of others. 15._____

16. It seems easy to perceive whether a person is honest or dishonest. 16._____
17. I am ready to try the impossible because I have a great trust in God. 17._____
18. There is great joy in having people in my home. 18._____
19. I find that the repair and maintenance of things in my environment comes easily to me. 19._____
20. I seem to recognize prayer needs before others. 20._____
21. I enjoy the opportunity to pray with and for a person who is physically ill that they may be made well. 21._____
22. I adapt easily in a culture different from mine. 22._____
23. I feel a sense of authority in my relationship to the group. 23._____
24. I like to proclaim the Word of God to comfort others. 24._____
25. I seem able to determine when the Spirit has prepared a person to receive Jesus Christ 25._____
26. It is exciting to provide spiritual leadership for a congregation. 26._____
27. Teaching a Bible class is one of the most enjoyable things I do (or could do) in the church. 27._____
28. God has given me the ability to play a musical instrument, and I enjoy it. 28._____
29. It is a joy to give encouragement to people who are discouraged. 29._____
30. I enjoy providing solutions to difficult problems in life. 30._____
31. It seems easy to learn difficult truths. 31._____
32. I enjoy doing routine tasks for the glory of God. 32._____
33. I enjoy helping with the emergency tasks around the church. 33._____
34. People seem to enjoy following me in doing an important task. 34._____
35. There is joy in making important decisions. 35._____
36. I find real joy in giving a generous portion of my money to the Lord. 36._____
37. Visiting people in retirement homes gives me a great satisfaction. 37._____
38. I seem to know very quickly whether something is right or wrong. 38._____
39. When things seem impossible, I'm ready to move forward. 39._____
40. I do not feel uncomfortable when people drop in unexpectedly. 40._____
41. I have enjoyed creating various kinds of arts and/or crafts. 41._____
42. Prayer is one of my favorite spiritual exercises. 42._____
43. I have prayed for an emotionally ill person and seen the person get better. 43._____
44. It is easy for me to move into a new community and make friends. 44._____
45. I have little fear in leading people where God wants them to go. 45._____
46. I enjoy relating and sharing God's Word to the issues of the day. 46._____
47. I feel a burden to share the gospel with people. 47._____
48. I like to assist people with their spiritual problems. 48._____
49. It seems that people learn when I teach them. 49._____

50. I have enjoyed being involved with church, school and/or local musical productions.   50._____
51. I like to encourage inactive church members to become involved Christians again.   51._____
52. It seems that people generally follow my advice.   52._____
53. I am able to understand difficult portions of God's Word.   53._____
54. I receive great satisfaction in doing small or trivial tasks in church.   54._____
55. I desire to do the tasks which will free others for important ministry.   55._____
56. It is more effective to delegate a task to someone else rather than to do it myself.   56._____
57. I enjoy the responsibility for the achievement of group goals.   57._____
58. I appreciate the opportunity to financially support a critical situation.   58._____
59. I sense joy in comforting people in difficult situations.   59._____
60. The difference between truth and error is easily perceived by me.   60._____
61. I am often ready to believe God will lead us through a situation when others feel it is impossible.   61._____
62. People seem to feel very comfortable in my home.   62._____
63. I like to create things with my hands.   63._____
64. God consistently answers my prayers in tangible ways.   64._____
65. I have visited a person who was sick, prayed that God would make them physically whole, and the person got better.   65._____
66. I am able to relate well to Christians of different locations or cultures.   66._____
67. I appreciate the opportunity to proclaim God's Word to others.   67._____
68. It is important for me to speak God's Word of warning and judgment in the world today.   68._____
69. It is a joy to share what Jesus means to me with an unchurched neighbor.   69._____
70. People like to bring their troubles and concerns to me because they feel I care.   70._____
71. One of the joys of my ministry is training people to be more effective Christians.   71._____
72. I feel secure in the fact that my musical ability will be of benefit to other people with whom I come in contact.   72._____
73. People who are feeling perplexed often come to me for encouragement and comfort.   73._____
74. I feel that I have a special insight in selecting the best alternative in a difficult situation.   74._____
75. I have a clear understanding of biblical doctrines (teachings).   75._____

76. I find more satisfaction in doing a job than finding someone 76._____
 else to do it.
77. I appreciate a ministry of helping other people to bear their burdens. 77._____
78. It is a thrill to inspire others to greater involvement in church work. 78._____
79. The development of effective plans for church ministry 79._____
 gives me great satisfaction.
80. It is a joy to see how much money I can give to the Lord. 80._____
81. I enjoy ministering to a person who is sick in the hospital. 81._____
82. I can judge well between the truthfulness and error of a 82._____
 given theological statement.
83. People seem to view me as one who believes everything is possible. 83._____
84. When missionaries come to our church I (would) like to 84._____
 have them come to my home.
85. I see that the results of my working with various objects in 85._____
 God's creation help to improve and beautify that which other people
 have not seen nor developed.
86. I faithfully pray for others recognizing that their 86._____
 effectiveness and total well-being depends on God's answer to prayers.
87. I like to participate in ministry to the physically or emotionally 87._____
 ill and pray for their recovery.
88. The thought of beginning a new church in a 88._____
 new community is exciting to me.
89. I enjoy training workers in the congregation. 89._____
90. In a Bible class, it seems essential to share God's Word even 90._____
 if it irritates others.
91. I feel a deep concern for the unreached people in my community. 91._____
92. I enjoy a close relationship with people in a one-to-one situation. 92._____
93. It is easy to organize materials for teaching a Bible class. 93._____
94. Leading others in singing songs of praise to God or for pure 94._____
 enjoyment is personally satisfying.
95. I would rather call on a delinquent family in my church than 95._____
 an unchurched family.
96. I have a strong sense of confidence in my solutions to problems. 96._____
97. It is an exciting challenge to read and study a difficult book of the Bible. 97._____
98. I like to do things without attracting much attention. 98._____
99. If a family is facing a serious crisis, I enjoy the opportunity to help them. 99._____
100. There is great satisfaction in having others follow me in 100._____
 performing a task.

101. I would rather make decisions for the group than persuade them   101._____
to reach the same decision.
102. I can give sacrificially because I know that God will meet my needs.   102._____
103. It is a special satisfaction to visit people who are confined to   103._____
their homes.
104. I often seek the motives of a person and look beneath the words.   104._____
105. When people are discouraged, I enjoy giving them a positive vision.   105._____
106. People seem to enjoy coming to my house.   106._____
107. There is pleasure in drawing, designing, and/or painting   107._____
various objects.
108. I find myself praying when I possibly should be doing other things.   108._____
109. I feel strongly that my prayers for a sick person affect   109._____
wholeness for that person.
110. More than most, I have a strong desire to see all people of other   110._____
communities and countries won to the Lord.

The Discovery Tool Profile Sheet

Transfer your scores for each question into the table on the following page, then compute the sum of each row.

PLEASE NOTE, The numbers on this sheet go VERTICALLY, in sequential order.
To score questions 1, 23, 45, 67 and 89, add them together horizontally,
giving you a grand total for the gift of Church Planter.
Continue this scoring through missionary gifts at the bottom of the table.
This provides your score for each gift.

1. Church Planter   1 ____ 23 ____ 45 ____ 67 ____ 89 ____ = ____
2. Prophet   2 ____ 24 ____ 46 ____ 68 ____ 90 ____ = ____
3. Evangelist   3 ____ 25 ____ 47 ____ 69 ____ 91 ____ = ____
4. Pastor   4 ____ 26 ____ 48 ____ 70 ____ 92 ____ = ____
5. Teacher   5 ____ 27 ____ 49 ____ 71 ____ 93 ____ = ____
6. Music   6 ____ 28 ____ 50 ____ 72 ____ 94 ____ = ____
7. Exhortation   7 ____ 29 ____ 51 ____ 73 ____ 95 ____ = ____
8. Wisdom   8 ____ 30 ____ 52 ____ 74 ____ 96 ____ = ____
9. Knowledge   9 ____ 31 ____ 53 ____ 75 ____ 97 ____ = ____
10. Serving   10 ____ 32 ____ 54 ____ 76 ____ 98 ____ = ____
11. Helps   11 ____ 33 ____ 55 ____ 77 ____ 99 ____ = ____
12. Leadership   12 ____ 34 ____ 56 ____ 78 ____ 100 ____ = ____
13. Administration   13 ____ 35 ____ 57 ____ 79 ____ 101 ____ = ____
14. Giving   14 ____ 36 ____ 58 ____ 80 ____ 102 ____ = ____
15. Mercy   15 ____ 37 ____ 59 ____ 81 ____ 103 ____ = ____
16. Discernment   16 ____ 38 ____ 60 ____ 82 ____ 104 ____ = ____
17. Faith   17 ____ 39 ____ 61 ____ 83 ____ 105 ____ = ____
18. Hospitality   18 ____ 40 ____ 62 ____ 84 ____ 106 ____ = ____
19. Craftsmanship   19 ____ 41 ____ 63 ____ 85 ____ 107 ____ = ____
20. Intercession   20 ____ 42 ____ 64 ____ 86 ____ 108 ____ = ____
21. Healing   21 ____ 43 ____ 65 ____ 87 ____ 109 ____ = ____
22. Missionary   22 ____ 44 ____ 66 ____ 88 ____ 110 ____ = ____

Name _____

The gifts I have begun to discover in my life are:

1._____

2._____

3._____

- After prayer and worship, I am beginning to sense that God wants me to use my spiritual gifts to serve Christ's body by _____.
- I am not sure yet how God wants me to use my gifts to serve others. But I am committed to prayer and worship, seeking wisdom and opportunities to use the gifts I have received from God.

Additional Resources

1. **Membership Matters - COGOP**
   - lddcogop.org
   - Resources > Membership Matters
2. **Leadership Development & Discipleship (LDD) In the COGOP**
   - *Visit lddcogop.org to find out more information*
3. **COGOP Governance & Doctrinal Documents for further doctrinal clarity**
   - *Visit cogop.org, hover over the "International Offices" tab, and then hover over "about us," from there explore the different options the Church has to offer for information.*

4. **A Free Spiritual Gifts Survey (Provided by Lifeway)**
   - *Scan this QR code with your phone, and access the survey*
   - *Share this with your group, and talk through it at the very end of this study.*

5. **A Free Understanding the Nature of the Gifts Guide (Provided by Lifeway)**
   - *Scan this QR code with your phone, and access the survey*
   - *Share this with your group, and talk through it at the very end of this study.*

COGOP Statement of Faith

We believe in the Holy Trinity—one God, eternally existing in Three Persons: Father, Son and Holy Spirit.

We believe in one God, the Father, creator of heaven and earth, of all things seen and unseen.

We believe in one Lord, Jesus Christ, the only Son of God, eternally begotten of the Father. All things were made through Him and for Him. He is true God and true man. He was conceived by the power of the Holy Spirit, and was born of the virgin Mary. He suffered, died, was buried, and on the third day He rose from the dead. He ascended to the right hand of the Father, and He will return to judge the living and the dead. His kingdom will have no end.

We believe in the Holy Spirit, the Lord and giver of life, who eternally proceeds from the Father. He is Teacher, Comforter, Helper and Giver of spiritual gifts. Through Him the saving and sanctifying works of Jesus Christ are applied to the life of believers. He is the empowering Presence of God in the life of the Christian and the Church. The Father has sent His Son to baptize with the Holy Spirit. Speaking in tongues and bearing the fruit of the Spirit are New Testament signs of being filled with the Holy Spirit.

We believe that salvation is by grace through faith in the sacrificial death of Jesus Christ on the cross; and that He died in our place. The believer's sins are forgiven by the shedding of His blood. We believe that healing of mind, body, soul and spirit is available to the believer through the blood of Jesus Christ, and the power of the Holy Spirit.

We believe in one baptism in the name of the Father and of the Son and of the Holy Spirit.

We believe that the grace of God brings forgiveness and reconciliation to those who repent, as well as transformation in holiness, enabling them to live a Christ-like life. Sanctification is both a definite work of grace, and a lifelong process of change in the believer brought by the blood of Jesus, the Word of God and the enabling power of the Holy Spirit.

We believe in one holy, universal Church, composed of all true believers in Jesus Christ, offering fellowship and calling for service to men and women of all peoples, nations, cultures and languages. We believe in the spiritual and ultimate visible unity of the Church

We believe that the Bible—both Old and New Testaments—is the inspired Word of God. The Bible is God's revelation of Himself and His will to humankind, sufficient for instruction in salvation and daily Christian living. The Bible is the Christian's rule of faith and practice.

We believe that God will ultimately reconcile all things in heaven and earth in Christ. Therefore, we look forward to new heavens and a new earth in which righteousness dwells.

COGOP Core Values

Prayer is the first of the Church of God of Prophecy's five core values. Prayer touches everything, informs all activities, empowers all ministry and service, and permeates the work from beginning to end. Jesus said, "It is written, my house is the house of prayer" (Matthew 21:13). Jesus gives no other description of his house anywhere. He does not talk about curtains or furniture or musical instruments. The Old Testament has a lot to say about what the tabernacle and the temple should look like and outlines in great detail the activities that are to take place in those houses of worship. Here, Jesus paints a picture for the not-as-yet-born church to see what his house is going to look like.

In 1994, the Holy Spirit clearly instructed the Church of God of Prophecy to "turn to **the harvest**." This was a critical moment for our movement. God had spoken to us, and his call would direct us. The reformations the Church of God of Prophecy experienced since then have solidified our determination to remain aligned with God's harvest priority. One simple result has been a growth in global ministry; worldwide membership is four times that of 1994. Today, the leadership of the Church of God of Prophecy holds God's Harvest call as a core value and a central mandate. It has not been rescinded or completely fulfilled. Neither can it be until all have heard.

Leadership Development is a third core value. The Church of God of Prophecy has used significant resources to create systems that cultivate a culture of excellence and produce competent, skilled leaders. The Church has created stable, reproducible results in its leadership training programs and built accountability into those programs. The Church has also significantly and measurably strengthened collaboration and connectedness among ministry leaders.

The fourth core value of the Church of God of Prophecy is **Biblical Stewardship**. The Church affirms that everything belongs to God. While he has graciously entrusted individuals with the care, development, and utilization of his resources, Christians are responsible to manage his holdings well and according to his desires and purposes. The Church acknowledges and encourages its members to recognize they are stewards of the resources, abilities, and opportunities God has entrusted to them, and one day, each one will be called to give an account for how what the Master gave was managed. Therefore, it is with joy that the Church works hand-in-hand with God, utilizing that which God had given, to his glory and honor.

The fifth core value of the Church of God of Prophecy is **Service**. Jesus served. He calls his followers to serve. All across the world, Church of God of Prophecy leaders, churches, and members serve their communities in a myriad of ways. They serve through community events, often partnering with charitable organizations to help those in need. Cleanup campaigns, emergency aid when disaster strikes, youth sports leagues, afterschool programs, care for the elderly, food pantries as well as teaching, preaching, giving, cooking, cleaning, helping, providing transportation—there are as many ways to serve as there are Church of God of Prophecy congregations. Our people serve.

References

Biblical Principles, Beliefs, and Practices of the Church of God of Prophecy. White Wing Publishing House, 2014, cogop.org/wp-content/uploads/2020/02/Biblical-Principles.pdf.

"Biblical Stewardship." *International Offices About* , cogop.org/core-values/.

Barry, John D., et al. *Lexham Bible Dictionary* . Edited by David Bomar, Lexham Press, 2016.

Foster, Richard J. *Celebration of Discipline*. Special Anniversary Edition, HarperOne, 2018.

Holt, Paul, and Barbara Holt. *The Goldfish Principle*. White Wing Publishing House, 2022.

Holy Bible, New American Standard Bible®, Copyright © 1960, 1971, 1977, 1995 by The Lockman Foundation

LifeWay Christian Resources. *Spiritual Gifts Assessment*. LifeWay Christian Resources, https://s7d9.scene7.com/is/content/LifeWayChristianResources/Spiritual_Gifts_Assessmentpdf.pdf. Accessed 25 Feb. 2025.

LifeWay Christian Resources. *Spiritual Gifts List*. LifeWay Christian Resources, https://s7d9.scene7.com/is/content/LifeWayChristianResources/Spiritual-Gifts-List-pdf.pdf. Accessed 25 Feb. 2025.

Sutton, Brian. *Join the Journey*. Brian Sutton, 2016, www.alcogop.org/_files/ugd/07a960_d8ba276014bc4a27b41cd4cce83b73ab.pdf.

S.O.A.P is a Bible Study method created by Wayne Cordero.

Webber, Robert. *Listening to the Beliefs of Emerging Churches* (Grand Rapids, MI: Zondervan, 2007).

About the Author

Ethan and His wife Shelby presently serve as the Pastors of Michie Church located in Michie, Tennessee. Prior to serving as lead pastors, Ethan served as the Associate Pastor at Union Grove Church of God of Prophecy in Mooreville, MS. Together, for a short time, they served as the Communication Pastors at Union Grove.

Ethan has both an Associates and Bachelors Degree in Music Education from Itawamba Community College in Fulton, MS and Mississippi State University in Starkville, MS. Presently, Ethan is pursuing a Master of Arts in Church Ministries / Discipleship & Ministry Leadership from the Pentecostal Theological Seminary in Cleveland, TN.

Made in the USA
Columbia, SC
07 May 2025